UGLY SISTERS

by Charli Cowgill and Laurie Ward

FOR AMATEUR PRODUCTION ENQUIRIES

UNITED KINGDOM AND WORLD
EXCLUDING NORTH AMERICA
licensing@concordtheatricals.co.uk
020-7054-7298

Each title is subject to availability from Concord Theatricals, depending upon country of performance.

The moral right of Charli Cowgill and Laurie Ward to be identified as author of this work has been asserted in accordance with Section 77 of the Copyright, Designs and Patents Act 1988.

USE OF COPYRIGHTED MUSIC

A licence issued by Concord Theatricals to perform this play does not include permission to use the incidental music specified in this publication. In the United Kingdom: Where the place of performance is already licensed by the PERFORMING RIGHT SOCIETY (PRS) a return of the music used must be made to them. If the place of performance is not so licensed then application should be made to PRS for Music (www.prsformusic.com). A separate and additional licence from PHONOGRAPHIC PERFORMANCE LTD (www.ppluk.com) may be needed whenever commercial recordings are used. Outside the United Kingdom: Please contact the appropriate music licensing authority in your territory for the rights to any incidental music.

USE OF COPYRIGHTED THIRD-PARTY MATERIALS

Licensees are solely responsible for obtaining formal written permission from copyright owners to use copyrighted third-party materials (e.g., artworks, logos) in the performance of this play and are strongly cautioned to do so. If no such permission is obtained by the licensee, then the licensee must use only original materials that the licensee owns and controls. Licensees are solely responsible and liable for clearances of all third-party copyrighted materials, and shall indemnify the copyright owners of the play(s) and their licensing agent, Concord Theatricals Ltd., against any costs, expenses, losses and liabilities arising from the use of such copyrighted third-party materials by licensees.

IMPORTANT BILLING AND CREDIT REQUIREMENTS

If you have obtained performance rights to this title, please refer to your licensing agreement for important billing and credit requirements.

NOTE

This edition reflects a rehearsal draft of the script and may differ from the final production.

UGLY SISTERS was first produced by piss / CARNATION at the Edinburgh Fringe Festival in August 2024. The performance was directed by Joanna Pidcock, with sets and costumes by Cara Evans, lighting design by Edward De'Ath, and sound design by MILKBOY. The Producer was Bronagh Leneghan, and the Production Stage Manager was Daze Corder. The cast was as follows:

GERMAINE GREER......................Charli Cowgill/Laurie Ward

FLAPPING DRAPERIES ....Charli Cowgill/Laurie Ward

STAGE MANAGER .... Daze Corder

New Diorama Theatre is a pioneering studio venue in the heart of London.

Based on the corner of Regent's Park, over the last ten years New Diorama has been at the heart of a new movement in British theatre. New Diorama is the only venue in the UK entirely dedicated to providing a home for the country's best independent theatre companies and ensembles, and has established a national record as a trailblazer for early-career artist support.

"A genuine theatrical phenomenon – a miniature powerhouse." – *The Stage*

In 2022, New Diorama was named *The Stage*'s Fringe Theatre Of The Year, for the second time in its short history; and in 2023 was awarded the inaugural Critics' Circle Empty Space Venue Award. Since opening in 2010, New Diorama's work has won four prestigious Peter Brook Awards; eleven Off West End Awards including Off West End Artistic Director of the Year; and *The Stage*'s Innovation Prize.

"A must-visit destination for London theatregoers." – *Time Out*

Work commissioned and produced at New Diorama frequently tours nationally and internationally, including regular transfers Off Broadway and co-curating New York's celebrated Brits Off Broadway Festival with 59E59 Theaters. *The Stage* 100, which charts power and influence across British Theatre, currently list New Diorama as the most influential independent studio theatre in the UK.

"A crucial part of the wider UK theatre ecology and an under-sung hero." – *The Guardian*

In 2023, New Diorama achieved a further milestone with two original commissions transferring into London's West End. *For Black Boys Who Have Considered Suicide When The Hue Gets Too Heavy*, originally co-produced with Nouveau Riche and earning their artistic director Ryan Calais-Cameron an Olivier Award nomination for Best New Play, transferred first to the Royal Court Theatre before sell-out West End runs at the Apollo Theatre and Garrick Theatre. Alongside, *Operation Mincemeat*, an original New Diorama commission from musical theatre company Spitlip, transferred to the Fortune Theatre, where it is currently playing an open-ended run after multiple extensions and has won the 2024 Olivier Award for Best New Musical.

"New Diorama has only been around for a decade but has already left a huge mark on the global theatre scene." – *WhatsOnStage*

www.newdiorama.com | @NewDiorama | New Diorama Theatre, 15-16 Triton Street, Regent's Place, London NW1 3BF.

Established in 2000, Underbelly is a UK-based live entertainment company specialising in programming and producing ground-breaking theatrical productions, cultural city centre events and original festivals.

Founded at the Edinburgh Festival Fringe by Ed Bartlam and Charlie Wood, Underbelly remains a pioneer of untapped talent across the world of theatre, comedy, circus and cabaret, entertaining audiences from London to Edinburgh, and Asia to North America.

As a leading venue producer at the Edinburgh Festival Fringe, Underbelly's 2024 programme will welcome over 160+ shows across 20 performances spaces. Notable highlights across our 24-year history at the festival include Phoebe Waller-Bridge's *Fleabag* in 2013, Marlow and Moss' *SIX* in 2018, Manual Cinema's *Ada/Ava* in 2016, 1927's *Between the Devil and the Deep Blue Sea* in 2007, Rob Madge's *My Son's A Queer (But What Can You Do?)* in 2022 and Francesca Moody Productions' *Kathy & Stella Solve a Murder!* in 2023.

On the West End, Underbelly is the lead and originating producer of the Olivier Award-winning revival of *Cabaret* at the Kit Kat Club, alongside ATG Productions, now in its third year and originally starring Eddie Redmayne and Jessie Buckley.

Expanding into new ventures, in 2023 Underbelly launched its first permanent venue, Underbelly Boulevard, in the heart of Soho. A vibrant and dynamic entertainment destination boasting a state-of-the-art auditorium, Underbelly Boulevard has hosted world-class cabaret, comedy, theatre and circus in its inaugural year including Bernie Dieter's *Club Kabarett*; Three Legged Race Productions' *Sophie's Surprise 29th*; John Bishop; Josh Thomas; Mason Alexander Park's *The Pansy Craze*; and Mario The Maker Magician.

Other current London festivals include Underbelly Festival at Cavendish Square, Christmas in Leicester Square and Christmas in Trafalgar Square; as well as proudly being the event production partner for West End Live in Trafalgar Square (on behalf of Westminster City Council and Society of London Theatre).

Underbelly recently partnered with Wessex Grove to produce the critically acclaimed production of *Macbeth* starring Ralph Fiennes and Indira Varma, as it toured to Liverpool (The Depot), Edinburgh (Royal Highland Centre), London (Dock X) and Washington DC (Shakespeare Theatre Company).

Other credits include The McOnie Company's *Nutcracker* at the Tuff Nutt Jazz Club (Southbank Centre), *Tweedy's Massive Circus* (UK Tour), *Five Guys Named Moe* (Marble Arch Theatre) Oliver Award-nominated for Best Entertainment; *Cabaret Royale* (Gaillard Centre, Charleston USA); and *La Clique* (London, Manchester and Singapore 2021).

www.underbelly.co.uk | @FollowTheCow | @underbellyedinburgh

Underbelly

Directors . . . . Ed Bartlam and Charlie Wood
PA to Directors and Office Manager . . . . Lauren Manning

Head of Programming and Producer . . . . .Marina Dixon
Senior Programmer . . . . .Aisling Galligan
Senior Producer. . . . . Áine Flanagan
Programme Coordinator . . . . Alex Cofield

Head of Marketing . . . . .Lauren Carroll
Marketing Manager . . . . Demi McAleer
Marketing Executive . . . . Hope Martin
Social Media and Content Officer . . . . Angus Livingstone

Head of Production. . . . . Ian Gibbs
Production Manager. . . . . Kenny Easson
Technical Manager . . . . .Andrew Gorman
Warehouse and Logistics Manager . . . . .Steven Kilpatrick
Production Coordinator. . . . . .Joe Ewing

Senior Event Producer. . . . . Ruth Fisher
Event Producer . . . . .Rachel Sivills-McCann
Executive Producer. . . . . Holly Reiss

Head of Operations. . . . . .Ryan Beattie
Operations Manager. . . . . .Joe Mills

Head of Ticketing . . . . .Natalie Norman
Head of Bars. . . . . Jonny Brown
Head of Brand Partnerships . . . . .Mary Gleeson
Head of Finance . . . . Jace Subramoney

UNTAPPED

UNDERBELLY | NEW DIORAMA THEATRE | CONCORD THEATRICALS

Originally developed in 2018 by New Diorama and Underbelly to discover and support emerging theatre makers at the Edinburgh Festival Fringe, the Untapped Award has established a remarkable record as a platform for bold new theatre by outstanding companies.

Over the last six years, the Untapped Award has provided a springboard for a diverse array of major Edinburgh Fringe premieres. Previous recipients have gone on to win three Fringe First Awards – *This is Not a Show About Hong Kong* (Max Percy & Friends); *It's True, It's True, It's True* (Breach); *Dressed* (ThisEgg) – and *The Stage* Edinburgh Award – *Queens of Sheba* (Nouveau Riche). Winners have also gone on to secure major national and international tours following the festival, including Side eYe Productions' *Dugsi Dayz* (Royal Court transfer), FlawBored's *It's A Motherf**king Pleasure* (*The Stage*'s The Fringe Five), Burnt Lemon's *Tokyo Rose*, Ugly Bucket's *Good Grief* and Nouveau Riche's *Queens of Sheba*, which most recently played at New York's Public Theater for the prestigious Under the Radar Festival; and adaptations for screen, with *It's True, It's True, It's True* broadcast on BBC television.

"The Untapped trio ranked among the best of the entire festival, proof that support from organisations like Underbelly and New Diorama can pay off in spades." – *WhatsOnStage*

In 2023, the award was relaunched and super-charged with support from new partner Concord Theatricals, with the cash investment in each company doubled to £10,000 alongside an extensive paid-for support package and publication by Concord Theatricals under their UK imprint Samuel French Ltd.

Drawn from a nationwide talent search, the three 2024 winners are *Ugly Sisters* by piss / CARNATION, an operatic, heretic and parasitic dissection of Germaine Greer, sisterhood and all feminist history; *The Mosinee Project* by Counterfactual, a fevered, darkly funny retelling of a true story about a fake Communist invasion in a small American town; and *DRUM* by Our Day, a joyful and poignant play capturing a unique snapshot of London's Ghanaian diaspora in the swinging sixties.

ABOUT piss / CARNATION

piss / CARNATION is an award-winning transfemme performance duo led by Charli Cowgill and Laurie Ward. Their anti-disciplinary work straddles performance art, new writing and queer cabaret. Their debut work *52 Monologues for Young Transsexuals* (Soho Theatre) has been praised as "brutally revealing and beautifully soft" (*Guardian* ****), "genuinely groundbreaking" (To Do List *****), and won an OFFIE Award for LGBTQ+ Performance at the Edinburgh Fringe Festival.

CAST

CHARLI COWGILL | Lead Artist

Charli Cowgill is a London-based performer, and writer for stage. She graduated in English from the University of Cambridge, and has since produced work as co-lead artist in piss / CARNATION. Her credits as writer and performer include:

52 Monologues for Young Transsexuals (Soho Theatre); *Ugly Sisters* (New Diorama Theatre, Untapped).

LAURIE WARD | Lead Artist

Laurie Ward is a transfeminine theatremaker, based in London, producing work as one half of piss / CARNATION. Her credits include *52 Monologues for Young Transsexuals* (Soho Theatre); *Ugly Sisters* (New Diorama Theatre, Untapped).

CREATIVE

JOANNA PIDCOCK | Director

Joanna Pidcock is a London-based Australian director, dramaturg, and writer. Her work as a Director includes *Ugly Sisters* for New Diorama and Underbelly Edinburgh, and *A Very Small Trouble* for Shakespeare's Globe (R&D). She was a finalist for the 2024 JMK Award, and longlisted for the 2019 Genesis Future Directors Award. As Associate Director: *The Confessions* for National Theatre and European Tour. As Assistant or Intern Director: *I, Joan* for Shakespeare's Globe; *Ravens* for Hampstead Theatre; *La Maladie de la mort* for Bouffes du Nord; and *Angels in America* for fortyfivedownstairs. As Movement Director: *Not Dying* at the Barbican Centre. Opera includes *How Was it For You* (co-director and librettist) at Toshima Civic Centre, Tokyo; *The Garden Party* (librettist) in development the Royal Opera House. She has worked as a librettist on a development residency with Britten Pears Arts, and as a dramaturg on a project in development with Katie Mitchell and Alice Birch at the Schaubühne. As an essayist, she was shortlisted for the 2021 Fitzcarraldo Editions Essay Prize.

CARA EVANS | Set and Costume Designer

Cara Evans (They/She) is a London-based performance designer. Cara graduated in Design for Stage from the Royal Central School of Speech and Drama and also worked as a reader for the Royal Court.

Theatre includes: as Designer or Co-Designer, *Feral Monster* (National Theatre Wales); *Sleepova* (Bush Theatre); *Dear Young Monster* (Bristol Old Vic Studio); *The Living Newspaper* (Royal Court); *Sirens* (Mercury Colchester Studio); *Get Dressed!* (Unicorn); *Queer Upstairs* (Royal Court); *Body Show* (SohoTheatre); *Sylvia* (English Theatre Frankfurt); *It's a Motherf**king Pleasure* (National Tour); *SK Shlomo: Breathe* (Royal Albert Hall); *F**king Men* (Waterloo East); *The Beach House* (Park Theatre Studio); *Love Bomb* (National Youth Theatre); *Baba Joon* (Swansea Grand Studio); *Bright Half Life* (King's Head); *The Misandrist* (Arcola); *Instructions for A Teenage Armageddon* (Southwark Playhouse); *Blanket Ban* (New Diorama, Untapped); *A Different Class* (Queen's Theatre Hornchurch); as Associate Designer for Chloe Lamford, *Teenage Dick* (Donmar School's Tour).

DAZE CORDER | Stage Manager

Daze Corder is a London-based Stage Manager and Showcaller with a particular interest in supporting new writing and devised work.

Theatre includes: *Jobsworth* (Pleasance Courtyard); *Everything I Own* (Brixton House); *The Ballad of Hattie and James* (Kiln Theatre); *52 Monologues for Young Transsexuals* (Soho Theatre).

BRONAGH LENEGHAN | Producer

Bronagh Leneghan is a Producer from Newcastle and currently based in London. She is piss / CARNATION's resident Producer and her credits include *52 Monologues for Young Transsexuals* (Soho Theatre); *Ugly Sisters* (New Diorama Theatre, Untapped).

EDWARD DE'ATH | Lighting Designer

Edward De'Ath is a London-based lighting designer and technical director/production manager. His recent credits include *52 Monologues for Young Transsexuals* (Soho Theatre); *Ugly Sisters* (New Diorama Theatre, Untapped); *We Remember The Fields As Wild* (Riverside Studios); *The Tempest* (European Tour).

MILKBOY | Sound Designer

MILKBOY (she/her) is Laurie Ward's nascent sound designer alter-ego. Her credits include *Ugly Sisters* (New Diorama Theatre, Untapped).

NAISSA BJØRN | Movement Director

Naissa is a movement director and dancer based in London. Previous credits for piss / CARNATION include *52 Monologues for Young Transsexuals* (Soho Theatre).

CHARACTERS

(by order of appearance)

GERMAINE GREER – F, multiple ages, played by a trans woman

FLAPPING DRAPERIES – F, multiple ages, played by a trans woman.

STAGE MANAGER – should be the production's actual stage manager

Other figures appear throughout the course of the play to be played by the two performers, such as the **MC** and the **BACKUP DANCER**. These are not characters as such, but figures of fantasy, forces of stagecraft, or human props in the scene.

AUTHORS' NOTE

Ugly Sisters draws inspiration from an article penned by Germaine Greer in 1989 entitled "On Why Sex Change Is A Lie". In this article, Greer depicts an interaction on the day *The Female Eunuch* was issued in America, in which a transgender woman rushes up to her and grabs her by the hand. We have never heard from this woman. It has only been possible to see her in the seconds on the page in which Greer gives her life: twenty years after the event. We do not know if she is still alive, or if she ever existed. When we read the text, we were restless to make sense of this interaction and this relationship. What emerged was something of an unrequited love story.

This work would not have been possible without the support we have received both from the Untapped Award and from Camden People's Theatre, New Diorama Theatre, Shoreditch Town Hall, and Underbelly. We want to thank Danielle James, Fran Charmaille, Joanna Ward, Roz Kaveney, and Travis Alabanza for their ingenuity and insight. We are also completely indebted to Joanna Pidcock, our director and dramaturg: Joanna, you are a force of erudition.

PROLOGUE

(Through the show's preset, **GERMAINE GREER** *and* **FLAPPING DRAPERIES** *stand across from one another, in silence.* **GERMAINE** *is clad in an Adult Human Females t-shirt, a grey pussycat wig, and pearls. She is inexplicably wearing eight-inch pleaser heels.* **FLAPPING** *is wearing an overly-prissy princess dress, with long synthetic hair extensions and a pair of false eyelashes. Her lips are separated with a pair of bright red "sissy lips".* **GERMAINE** *is holding a leaf blower. They are locked in one another's gaze, teeming both with a sense of eroticism and violence.)*

("L.O.V.E." by SOPHIE plays. * *Smoke is pumped into the space as captions are projected along with the sound of the bass:)*

(Projected:)

[In 1970, legendary feminist Germaine Greer publishes The Female Eunuch. *It quickly emerges as a revolutionary, era-defining work of feminist thought.]*

---

* A licence to produce *Ugly Sisters* does not include a performance licence for "L.O.V.E." by SOPHIE. The publisher and author suggest that the licensee contact PRS to ascertain the music publisher and contact such music publisher to license or acquire permission for performance of the song. If a licence or permission is unattainable for "L.O.V.E.", the licensee may not use the song in *Ugly Sisters* but should create an original composition in a similar style or use a similar song in the public domain. For further information, please see the Music and Third-Party Materials Use Note on page iii.

[On the day The Female Eunuch *is issued in America.]*

[Germaine Greer speaks in a Town Hall debate.]

[On the day of the debate, she meets a transgender woman.]

(**GERMAINE** *begins to blow the leaf blower at* **FLAPPING**. *It is like* The Birth of Venus *restaged as a low-budget music video.)*

[The transgender woman grabs her hand.]

[(thank you)]

[(thank you so much for)]

[Twenty years later, Germaine Greer recounts the meeting in an article. The words you are about to hear come from this article, unedited.]

[The article is titled:]

["ON WHY SEX CHANGE IS A LIE"]

(The final slide stays on screen, begins flashing, glitching, as **GERMAINE** *points the leaf blower down, underneath* **FLAPPING**'s *dress and tries to upskirt her with something between curiosity and malice.* **FLAPPING** *uses her hands to stop the dress flashing: Marilyn Monroe.)*

ACT ONE

Germaine

(**GERMAINE** *begins to dictate from the article just mentioned.* **FLAPPING** *is stirred by Germaine's words into movement, as if Frantic Assembly had choreographed Germaine's memory. She appears like a horrible creature emerging from the depths.*)

(**FLAPPING** *exposes her breasts and shakes them. She is donning women's liberation nipple tassles.*)

(**FLAPPING** *bows her head and continues to jiggle her breasts offstage.*)

(**GERMAINE** *steps to the front of the stage. She gives a thumbs-up to the technician.*)

(*An audio retrospective on the career of* **GERMAINE GREER** *plays.* * *She listens, proudly, to content relating to her meteoric rise as a feminist in the 70s. But the audio begins to become fixated on her transphobia, and becomes corrupted. At this stage,* **FLAPPING** *enters, tip-toeing on with a leaf blower and*

---

* A licence to produce *Ugly Sisters* does not include a performance license for any third-party or copyrighted recordings. Licensees should create their own.

a thirst for vengeance. **GERMAINE** *becomes aware of* **FLAPPING**, *stupefied by her presence. This wasn't supposed to happen.* **GERMAINE** *attempts to escape from the clutches of her enormous, knuckley, hairy, be-ringed paws, but it is too late. The tragic fall of* **GERMAINE GREER** *has been set into motion:)*

*(***FLAPPING** *kills* **GERMAINE** *with the leaf blower.)*

(The house lights go up. This wasn't supposed to happen. **FLAPPING** *is mortified.)*

*(***FLAPPING** *looks to the* **AUDIENCE** *for help.)*

FLAPPING. Oh my God. No guys – this isn't – this wasn't – oh my God. Will somebody help me? We have to do something – I mean it's Germaine. Her body – it's going to bake under the stage lights.

*(***FLAPPING** *tells the audience she is responsible for burying* **GERMAINE***'s body and needs the* **AUDIENCE***'s help. She gestures toward a plot of earth in the corner. She picks out a couple of* **AUDIENCE MEMBERS** *to process* **GERMAINE***'s dead body around the theatre, ceremonially. She goes to the mic to sing "Dido's Lament", but she has changed the lyrics to one word: Germaine. Once* **GERMAINE** *is lowered into the Earth,* **FLAPPING** *gives the* **AUDIENCE** *bags of dirt. One by one, the* **AUDIENCE** *throws the dirt over* **GERMAINE***'s body to bury her.* **FLAPPING** *goes to give a eulogy.)*

On the day that *The Female Eunuch* was issued in America, I met Germaine Greer. She was everything you saw on the television: electric and daunting and pure steel.

So I was quite nervous, actually, when I met her! I'd dolled up – I mean, *really* dolled up – because I thought – there is no way I am going to let *Germaine Greer* see me with a face full of stubble. I even put on a pair of false eyelashes.

She smiled, which I wasn't expecting. I mean – *Germaine Greer*. You always saw her debating ruthlessly with men. And in the end, they would always submit. I forgot that a woman that intelligent had to be kind. Thank you, I said to her, thank you so much for everything you've done for us girls.

(She goes to seal the coffin.)

Goodnight, Germaine.

(She picks up a fistful of soil.)

We weren't ready for you.

(She chucks soil onto **GERMAINE***, with disrespect. Lights slowly fade onto the coffin.)*

*(***GERMAINE*** is resurrected. She lip syncs to the voice of Alyssa Edwards:*)*

*("Purrr" by Slayyyter begins.*** **GERMAINE** *serves pure, unadulterated cunt. At some point, a* **BACKUP DANCER** *enters [who*

---

* A licence to produce *Ugly Sisters* does not include a performance license for any third-party or copyrighted recordings. Licensees should create their own.
** A licence to produce *Ugly Sisters* does not include a performance licence for "Purrr" by Slayyyter. The publisher and author suggest that the licensee contact PRS to ascertain the music publisher and contact such music publisher to license or acquire permission for performance of the song. If a licence or permission is unattainable for "Purrr", the licensee may not use the song in *Ugly Sisters* but should create an original composition in a similar style or use a similar song in the public domain. For further information, please see the Music and Third-Party Materials Use Note on page iii

> *formerly played* **FLAPPING***] in a matching
> Adult Human Females tee. It is a TERF lip
> sync extravaganza. They end in a fierce
> pose. The house lights come up. The* **STAGE
> MANAGER** *enters with two stools. It turns
> out that the* **BACKUP DANCER** *is actually the*
> **MC** *of a conference.* **GERMAINE** *sits with the*
> **MC***. Some ad-lib ensues – "could we get some
> microphones in here; thank you" etc. They are
> setting up for a Q&A.)*

MC. Germaine Greer – thank you so much for what we just
saw. To introduce, quickly, Germaine Greer is a thinker
who has left an indelible mark on feminist criticism.
Her seminal work *The Female Eunuch* was published in
1970 and quickly emerged as a revolutionary manifesto
in feminist thought. Known for her sharp wit, Greer
is an internationally esteemed – and feared! – debater
and speaker. Germaine Greer – welcome.

GERMAINE. Thank you.

MC. Could you tell everyone a little more about what we
just saw?

GERMAINE. Well – it's an interpretive dance and spoken
word piece about perspective.

> *(Pregnant pause.)*

Could I get a glass of water?

> *(The* **STAGE MANAGER***, quickly, unrealistically
> quickly, brings a glass of water.* **GERMAINE**
> *takes a sip,* **MC** *goes to speak, and* **GERMAINE**
> *continues.)*

Marx has a saying for it – that everything happens
twice. The first time is tragedy; the second is farce.
Now that's neither here nor there, but the difference
between those two is perspective. And the first time

this happened to me I was really quite – disturbed. So I thought – if I make this a second time, with that distance from the event, then really I'll be able to laugh.

MC. It strikes me that humour, or laughter, as you say, is important to your work?

GERMAINE. Well yes! I mean – laughter, frankly, is a function of catharsis. So when we're laughing, we're purging something quite nasty out of us.

MC. And what are you calling the piece?

GERMAINE. I'm calling it – *Mrs Doubtfire*.

MC. So what was the impetus for this piece – why did you create this work – why now?

GERMAINE. Well, there is something deeply dissociative about being a feminist in today's climate.

MC. Can we speak more about that, now?

GERMAINE. Well because on the one hand, since I begun getting asked about transgenderism in the mainstream, I kind of, became blacklisted, in a sense. But at the same time – I was also asked to come and speak a lot more in that period, in the transgender tipping point, as it were – But really, I just don't care about all of that!

MC. I think that that frustration really comes out in the work.

GERMAINE. Well theatre is ephemeral. But I really wanted to stage this – this scandal – that femininity – the big hair, the false eyelashes, the poofy dress – is being repackaged and sold to us as the real deal. When we – you and me – we all know that it's not! And so I wanted to stage this fall – not just the fall in *my* experience, but also in *standards*. And it is that person who gets the last word. And gets to throw the dirt on me.

MC. But then you come alive.

GERMAINE. Right.

MC. Which is you offering a sense of hope?

GERMAINE. Well – that these people are not going to put a stop to me living my life. I refuse to be buried. I am a woman!

MC. Right. We are women.

GERMAINE. And there are parts of that experience that *can't* be de- or re-gendered. You know, we went through female puberty, and this change even continues to characterise us as women – there is a distinctly sonic dimension to gender, for instance. And we never talk about it, but there is a fact that when all of us speak, our voices produce a frequency – and a pitch – and a resonance. Because the larynx – it changes during puberty. There is that ephemerality again, that I was speaking about. And strangely this ephemerality simultaneously unites and divides people – where, for example – everyone can see that you've got tits, you've got a bloody marvellous fringe, your cheeks have filled out nicely from I would guess one to three years of synthetic estrogen, but as soon as I hear your voice I experience a particular moment. Aristotle had a word for it, in fact – he called it *anagnorisis*. It means recognition – it means a change from ignorance to knowledge. And in that moment, when you speak, I know that you are a man.

> (*The* **MC** *looks ill. What did they just say? Did I just hear that correctly?* **GERMAINE** *smiles, as if completely undisturbed by the rhythm of her own speech.*)

And this is very interesting to me – and something I was talking about years and years ago – nearly fifty years ago, can you believe that, in *The Female Eunuch*. As soon as you make an utterance – a speech-act, so to speak, there is a literal yet ephemeral dimension of gender which is opened up – or a possibility that is closed down – and a truth that is illuminated. In short, you look to be the husk, or skin, of a woman, and as soon as that body becomes lived in, agential, active, you become a man. And there is simply no escaping that.

Sorry, can I have a glass of water?

> *(The world dips, momentarily, into that of* Rupaul's Drag Race. **GERMAINE** *is ventriloquised by the voice of Shangela.* **FLAPPING** *is ventriloquised by the voice of Mimi Imfurst.* The two play out a backstage confrontation, where Shangela tells Mimi that she'll never be glamour.* **GERMAINE** *is telling* **FLAPPING***: you'll never make it.)*

> *(Pause.)*

Excuse me

> *(***GERMAINE** *calls the* **STAGE MANAGER.***)*

Does he know he isn't supposed to be in here?

> *(A pause.)*

I mean it's okay. You can stay. Why don't you go back to your seat for me?

> *(***FLAPPING** *stands. The* **STAGE MANAGER** *takes away the chair, suddenly. It is as if* **FLAPPING** *never had one to begin with.* **GERMAINE** *smiles at how pitiful* **FLAPPING** *is.)*

FLAPPING. I just – just wanted to say thank you for all you've done for us girls.

> *(***FLAPPING** *looks around in confusion.* **GERMAINE** *points to the sissy lips.)*

---

* A licence to produce *Ugly Sisters* does not include a performance license for any third-party or copyrighted transcripts or perfromances. Licensees should create their own.

GERMAINE. Are you looking for these?

(**FLAPPING** *shakes her head no.*)

These are your lips.

(**FLAPPING** *puts on the lips, accepting the thing* **GERMAINE** *says she is.*)

(*As soon as the lips are secured,* **GERMAINE** *removes her wig, gets up, lights change.* **STAGE MANAGER** *re-enters and begins to disassemble the set. The* **STAGE MANAGER** *removes the Adult Human Females tee and the princess dress from* **FLAPPING***. This reveals a corset and a skirt-cage around* **FLAPPING***, under which she is fully naked. Soil covers the stage. It is as if the lips are delivering something poisonous into* **FLAPPING***, and she begins to feel something contorting her from the inside: first her face, then chest, then stomach, then she is lashing herself from side to side. When she throws her torso down, she sees a monstrous exoskeleton around her body – she desperately tries to escape it – and succeeds, throwing it off behind her before collapsing –*)

–

–

(*But it was not enough – she needs to escape her body itself – she feels like she is dying – she is contorting – retching – becoming something completely alien to herself – she can't breathe, she is dancing the dance of death, dipping, splitting, twirling, accept the name, left behind, bow your head, pina, bausch, desperation, until –*)

(The **STAGE MANAGER** *puts* **FLAPPING** *out of her misery with a confetti gun.)*

ACT TWO

(**FLAPPING** *lies crumpled in a pile on the ground.* **FLAPPING** *speaks, still catching her breath.*)

FLAPPING. I just wanted to say thank you – when I saw her – across the crowd – coming out the doors of the Town Hall – she had this – pull – you know – this – pull – gravitational 'cause well – she's Germaine Greer – she was everything you saw on the television – she was ruthless – and brilliant – and in that room – every woman in that room – we felt like we'd won.

I wanted to thank her. For giving me that feeling.

I just wanted her to know that we were on the same side. 'Cause I'd spent the whole day braiding my hair – picking my dress – doing my makeup – spending hours shaving – all of this to – I just thought – there is no way I'm going to let Germaine Greer see me with a full face of stubble – but then when she looked at me it was like my voice it was – I felt caught and – I didn't want her to hear – I wanted to sound – I just needed to – say something – quickly – quickly – so I said

thank you

And I walked home thinking god – you idiot – Germaine Greer! – to simply thank her – so many more things I could say like – tell her like – I could have told her about – how I found her for the first time.

When I read her pamphlet. Or heard her speak on *Desert Island Discs*. When I heard her podcast on Spotify. When I saw her town hall debate on the TV

– with my mum – this blistering intellect – a total star
– ruining men in a shag mullet –

and her prose, I mean my God! It's not even that
I knew what the book meant, really, when I read it the
first time, – it took me six months to get through it and
by the end I still didn't even know what a eunuch was.
I was nowhere in that book but somehow, she spoke
straight to me. I used to read my favourite passages in
The Female Eunuch to my mum - and when it came to
telling her, it's like she remembered by intuition what
you wrote when you said that being a woman costs you
your life, because she asked me why I would choose a
life with more pain. It took us a while to really see each
other but we did!

We did! We talked and cried and she read *The
Transgender Issue* which helped, actually, and
she cried more and said but you might never
be able to be a teacher cuz Shon Faye she says
trans women have hard times in schools and
I cried, too, and said Mum, when have I ever wanted
to be a teacher? And she laughed and she remembered
me and I started telling her everything!

And she told me things too, and Germaine, it's like
our lives, they had been so remote, and they opened
up to each other! Through what... The *feeling* of
womanhood? Is that what we are united by Germaine?
The rapes that we call bad sex? The weirdness? The
secret, sacred joys?

I worry that we have nothing but our words. I know
you do too – you worry and you share your worry with
the world and I think it is brave and when people call
you dangerous, or insensitive – they're missing that
really – you are complete sensitivity. You're sensitive
and attuned, to the sound of things, the sound of power.

Does it make you lonely, being so sensitive? ...When
you're not on YouTube or behind a panel – I mean in

private, in your garden with your hands in the soil – who sees you, Germaine? I want to – to ask questions and talk – about – about your marriage that lasted for three weekends and how you cast off the recognition of the Man – how you learned to be uncompromising and if I might be able to learn too – I want – I want – to just – lie together and talk – and –

> (**GERMAINE** *has materialised, quite out of nowhere.* **FLAPPING** *does not quite see* **GERMAINE**, *until she has fully materialised over the following lines: forged out of the force of her language, and the desire for a comrade.*)

GERMAINE. Talk.

FLAPPING. And talk! And ask questions just –

GERMAINE. – Talking –

FLAPPING. – about life – our lives – just –

GERMAINE. – Talking –

FLAPPING. So that I – could tell you that

I feel like I know you...

GERMAINE. *(Playfully.)* Well you don't –

FLAPPING. I know

GERMAINE. – Know me

FLAPPING. No

GERMAINE. But you want to. You want to know me

FLAPPING. Yes

GERMAINE. You want a friend.

You want to be my friend

FLAPPING. ...yeah

GERMAINE. A sister –

> (**FLAPPING** *shrugs, coyly.*)

A Fairy Godmother?

FLAPPING. I'm not a child.

GERMAINE. Not quite.

FLAPPING. How old are you.

GERMAINE. I'm eighty-five.

FLAPPING. And how old do you think I am

GERMAINE. I have no idea how old you are.

You look young, but tired, in a timeless sort of way.

You know, you've got one of those faces.

Pre-raphaelite, in a way

And in this light, quite genderless

FLAPPING. What do you want?

GERMAINE. No one's asked me that in a while

Reach a certain age and people stop asking you about the things you want

I want to see my roses through winter.

To be genuinely stirred.

To escape polite conversation once and for all.

And for one more spellbinding fuck.

How's that?

FLAPPING. And nothing of sexual revolution?

GERMAINE. I'm getting tired

> (*Pause.*)

Aren't you tired?

FLAPPING. Yeah.

GERMAINE. It tires you out. The maintenance

FLAPPING. The image

GERMAINE. But then in moments

FLAPPING. Small moments

GERMAINE. In quiet corners

FLAPPING. I look into myself

GERMAINE. Over myself

FLAPPING. My body –

GERMAINE. My work –

FLAPPING. And I'm not sure –

GERMAINE. that I'm anywhere closer –

FLAPPING. After all these years –

GERMAINE. to *knowing* –

FLAPPING. what being a woman –

GERMAINE. *feels* like.

> (**FLAPPING** *and* **GERMAINE** *look into one another's eyes. It is as if they finally see one another.*)

FLAPPING. Roses, to be stirred, escape politeness, a spellbinding fuck.

GERMAINE. And remind me, exactly, *what it is that you want.*

> (**FLAPPING** *hesitates.*)

FLAPPING. I want to know what sex will be like after the revolution.

("Bipp" by SOPHIE plays. * **GERMAINE** *and* **FLAPPING** *fuck. And it is electrifying. It is the hottest sex imaginable. They ripple, twist, lick, grind, and seem totally attuned to the desires of the other. They take their wigs off and it is like they are revealing themselves, or removing distinguishing features so that they can become one body. The fucking gets playful and romantic in its childishness: they spit water at one another and chase each other around the stage – before falling back into kissing. But somehow, there's something about it that isn't really working anymore. After the genuine romance and playfulness, it feels too real. They try to keep kissing. The song ends. They mutter and mumble and the audience hear the sounds of making out. It feels like they are in front of one another as bodies now, and it is impossibly banal.)*

(Through fucking, **GERMAINE** *and* **FLAPPING** *have swapped bodies. Now the performer who played* **GERMAINE** *in the first half plays* **FLAPPING***, and vice versa. The audience doesn't clock this until* **GERMAINE** *gets dressed.)*

FLAPPING. That was great.

...

GERMAINE. Yeah.

---

* A licence to produce *Ugly Sisters* does not include a performance licence for "Bipp" by SOPHIE. The publisher and author suggest that the licensee contact PRS to ascertain the music publisher and contact such music publisher to license or acquire permission for performance of the song. If a licence or permission is unattainable for "Bipp", the licensee may not use the song in *Ugly Sisters* but should create an original composition in a similar style or use a similar song in the public domain. For further information, please see the Music and Third-Party Materials Use Note on page iii.

...

...

...

FLAPPING. *(Playfully, referencing the spitting.)* I should probably get you some more water.

GERMAINE. No – it's fine.

...

...

...

FLAPPING. Or your top?

GERMAINE. Honestly – it's fine.

FLAPPING. It gets cold in here – gets cold in here cuz we don't really have proper heating and obviously – it's a massive room so –

GERMAINE. I should go.

...

I think

...

FLAPPING. Okay.

...

> (**GERMAINE** *starts to move.*)

Are you sure?

Just because I –

GERMAINE. Yeah. Sorry. This was great.

> (**GERMAINE** *begins to gather her things. The gathering takes a while. It feels grisly.*)

GERMAINE. ...

  ...

  ...

  ...

> (**GERMAINE** *puts her Adult Human Females
> top on, facing away from* **FLAPPING**. *As soon
> as it falls over her torso,* **FLAPPING** *blurts:)*

FLAPPING. I saw what you wrote about me.

  ...

I read it.

  ...

GERMAINE. I have no idea what you're talking about.

FLAPPING. A person in flapping draperies?

> (**GERMAINE** *has been caught red-handed.)*

I read it. It was horrendous. I mean – it was really...
awful. It breathed hoarsely? My stubble burgeoning?

  ...

  ...

You wrote about me. After twenty years.

GERMAINE. Not quite twenty years

FLAPPING. Was I on your mind that entire time?

GERMAINE. Closer to eighteen, I think.

FLAPPING. Please don't be pedantic right now.

GERMAINE. And a half.

FLAPPING. But you accept that you said it.

GERMAINE. Well – I didn't say it.

FLAPPING. They were your words.

GERMAINE. I wrote it.

FLAPPING. *(Snapping.)* You said it! You wrote that – about me. Do you not understand that the things you say hurt people.

GERMAINE. *(Pure apathy.)* Sorry. It was rhetorical flourish. It can't actually hurt anyone. I'm sorry. OK?

(**FLAPPING** *is enraged.*)

FLAPPING. You turned me into a freak.

GERMAINE. I kept you anonymous. I didn't turn you into anything!

FLAPPING. I reached my hand out towards you.

GERMAINE. You grabbed onto me.

FLAPPING. I wanted to be your sister.

GERMAINE. And I don't know what makes you think that I owe you my sorority.

FLAPPING. Why are you so mean?

GERMAINE. Oh come on.

FLAPPING. No – genuinely. Why are you so mean? Because you know it doesn't make you sound very clever. Even in your article – usually your prose is clear and lucid and brilliant – you are *so* intelligent – and that article – it is a fucking mess. That article *sucks* Germaine – and I thought maybe between the vitriol you could stretch to some genuine critique but –

I make you stupid, don't I? I make you stupefied – and you just have no idea what to do with me.

Because if you had *really* wanted to write about me – you would have had to write about a womanhood which means agency. And you would have seen that it could be fun and joyful and it could be *chosen* and it would mean that you would have to rewrite a lot of *The Female Eunuch*. Or at least add a hefty new chapter. And you know how that chapter would begin? It would begin on the day *The Female Eunuch* was issued in America – and the story of how you met me – a woman who fills her body with newness – who changes – who asserts desire – who loves beauty – who crosses the threshold of possibility.

> (**GERMAINE** *looks stupefied, as if* **FLAPPING** *is raving.*)

GERMAINE. Everything about you represents the *limits* of possibility.

> (*This is a mortifying blow.* **FLAPPING** *looks like she might burst into tears.*)

…

…

Listen, I get it.

It's magnificent being radical, isn't it?

It's a great feeling, but it isn't *real*.

I'm trying to tell you – that being a woman – it *won't* make you happy.

This will not make your life better.

You're what – twenty? Of course! Being a woman – it *is* fun when you're twenty – and it does feel like agency – and joy – and pleasure. But then suddenly.

You are an *old woman*. You turn on the TV, and what do you see? David Walliams and Matt Lucas playing old tarts! *Mrs Brown's Boys*! Old, hairy-arsed malefactors slapped up in a lick of paint. Am I supposed to believe that now I'm no longer a hot fuck, I may as well be a man? Am I supposed to recognise myself in a hairy transvestite?

FLAPPING. Of course not –

> (**GERMAINE** *takes the bag of soil and dumps it, in one fell swoop, over* **FLAPPING**.)

GERMAINE. I refuse to be buried.

> (*The lighting shifts into something gorgeous and completely concentrated on* **FLAPPING**. **FLAPPING** *smiles, covered in dirt. She addresses the* **STAGE MANAGER**, *or – nobody.*)

FLAPPING. And I would tell you that burials can nurture. I would tell you that I might be buried but that I am growing upwards in daylight. And you would roll your eyes. And you would tell me that I speak with too many metaphors. You'd tell me that you just don't want me to waste my life

– labouring under a delusion that things will change. And I'd tell you that sometimes I feel like I'm suffocating too. And you'd look across my body and remember that once, you believed in liberation. And you'd ask me if I'm trapped in the wrong body, how can I possibly become free.

And then I would say something like –

Well actually, that the wrong body is mostly a metaphor, anyway. And as an intelligent woman you really should have sensed that. Or not a metaphor – but – a scaffold, maybe, to help put words to a desire – or a feeling – so impossible it makes language crumble.

And you would wonder how we could ever defend ourselves, if we didn't have our words.

And I'd tell you that maybe there are moments when we don't need the words. We already know where the words are going.

And isn't that a solace? Maybe I wouldn't even need to tell you thank you, because we'd both already know. Maybe all it would take would be a look, and we would know each other.

FLAPPING. Although –

> *(She steps into her dress, being offered to her by the* **STAGE MANAGER***. She pulls it up to her waist. The fantasy dissipates.*

Or maybe it wouldn't be very likely anyway.

> *(The* **STAGE MANAGER** *helps her to get her arms in the dress.)*

Or I wouldn't have that much time.

> *(The* **STAGE MANAGER** *leaves.)*

Wait, did they just leave without zipping my dress up?

> *(She looks out to the wings.)*

Hey!

> *(The* **STAGE MANAGER** *is not coming back. She looks out to the audience for help.)*

> *(***FLAPPING** *finds a* **MEMBER OF THE AUDIENCE** *to help zip up her dress; ideally an older, cisgender woman. Then,* **FLAPPING** *remembers that she needs to do her hair, and asks for more help getting ready because today is a big day for her.)*

> *(They go onstage together to get* **FLAPPING** *ready. They have a private exchange which is inaudible beneath a relatively loud ambient score: it is pure image.*)*

---

* A licence to produce *Ugly Sisters* does not include a performance license for any third-party or copyrighted music. Licensees should create an original composition or use music in the public domain. For further information, please see the Music Use Note on page iii.

(A portrait of care transitions into something stranger.)

*(**FLAPPING** asks for hair extensions, lashes, and she begins to look ridiculous. A certain humanity slips away from her and yet – she feels beautiful.)*

*(**FLAPPING** realises that she is missing her lips. The **WOMAN** picks the lips up for her.)*

*(**FLAPPING** puts on the lips.)*

*(She smiles, unaware of herself. She thanks the **AUDIENCE MEMBER**, and goes to hug her.)*

*(**GERMAINE** appears. Through the force of her language, she frames the hug within her article: "On Why Sex Change is a Lie". Through the article being read, the **WOMAN** who was helping **FLAPPING** get ready is recast as Germaine Greer. She picks up where she left off at the beginning of the play.)*

*(**GERMAINE** leaves.)*

ACT THREE

(*Now, it is the day* The Female Eunuch *is issued in America: the time of* **GERMAINE**'s *article. And the day that* **FLAPPING** *had been getting ready for.*

(*The* **AUDIENCE MEMBER** *is invited to leave the stage. It is as if the Town Bloody Hall is over, and* **GERMAINE** *is just about to step into the car and leave. At which point,* **FLAPPING** *rushes through the stage and grabs her hand. She says:*)

FLAPPING. I just wanted to say thank you. Thank you so much for all you've done for us girls.

(**FLAPPING** *drops back away from her, proud, if a bit underwhelmed. Once the* **AUDIENCE MEMBER** *is off the stage, another* **FLAPPING** *runs past the first* **FLAPPING**, *bumping her shoulder. She wanted to say thank you, too, but has just missed her. She is dressed in an identical dress, only in a different colour. Despondent, she turns around and sees* **FLAPPING**.)

(*The* **FLAPPINGS** *see one another, merely for a few seconds on the street, yet it is like time opens. They are in disbelief, as if discovering another of their species. Seeing one another, it is as if they remember something vital. They look at one another as a way of seeing themselves, offering their own bodies as a* *way for the other to see – and be seen. They pull their hair back, move and stretch, in an act of generosity and curiosity.)*

(In this act they become aware of their hair extensions. Up until now, this had merely been their hair. Their fingers clasp the clips – miraculously, the extensions come loose. In disbelief, they hold them in their hands – and suddenly, in unison, drop them. We just did that. Then, again, until they are free entirely of the hair extensions.)

(What follows next is the eyelashes – then the dresses. They remove everything, until their bodies are laid bare.)

(They stand and look at one another's naked bodies, and they recognise it.)

(Then, they get dressed again. But this time, they redress in normal clothes which share the colour of their former flapping draperies. It is like they have shed a skin, they're not really **FLAPPINGS** *anymore, as much as two real trans women who have run into each other unexpectedly. Between those countless other bodies on the street, it is these two that share a history: despite having never known one another. If they were to speak – ...)*

(When they are ready, time closes back down. We return to that split-second, real-life moment on the street.)

(There is everything and nothing to say.)

(They part ways.)

End

9 780573 000621